What Do I Say?

How to Support Others in Grief

Catherine Hodge, LMHC

Print ISBN: 979-8-218-15221-5
Ebook ISBN: 979-8-218-15222-2

Book design by Sarah E. Holroyd
(https://sleepingcatbooks.com)

Illustrations by Jill Greenbaum

To my clients who have allowed
me to witness their pain and have
taught me about courage, resilience,
and the endurance of love.

CONTENTS

Acknowledgments

I never thought I would write a book. I don't enjoy writing, so this book would not have been possible without my informal editing and cheerleading team of Linda, Melissa, Julie, and Randi. I am forever grateful for your time and encouragement.

This book is beautiful because of my illustrator, Jill Greenbaum, and my book designer, Sarah Holroyd. Thank you for your talents!

Finally, thank you to my husband, Chip, who supports me in everything. I am still smitten. I love you.

INTRODUCTION

Do you know what to say to a close friend who lost her husband or how to support a colleague who lost his son to suicide? If you don't, you're not alone. Many people struggle with how to respond and realize they aren't equipped with the proper tools to support their friend or loved one in grief.

Over the past ten years, I have worked as a licensed mental health therapist supporting people grieving many types of losses and noticed a pattern. A significant obstacle to healing is the lack of a support system familiar with a healthy grieving process.

Despite someone's best intentions, misplaced or unexpressed words and actions can damage long-term relationships, especially during grief. This book is for people who want to support their grieving friend or loved one but don't know how.

WHAT IS GRIEF?

Grief is the natural process of adapting to a significant loss. Some typical examples of losses include:

* Death of a family member, a pet, a partner, a friend, a mentor, or a colleague
* Loss of a relationship (divorce, break-up from a partner or friendship)
* Loss of a job (laid off or retirement)
* Loss of a home, living situation, or important asset (due to natural disaster or crime)

- Loss of a pregnancy/child (miscarriage, adoption, or abortion)
- Loss of health (normal aging or serious medical diagnosis)
- Loss of identity due to life events (trauma, menopause, infertility, hormone changes, empty nester, marriage, or having children)
- Loss of a dream (having children, planned career path, or getting married)

Grief is a human experience, a life passage, a transition from the world of the known and familiar to the unknown. Everyone has experienced or will experience loss in their lifetime. Grieving is a part of our shared humanity.

Normal reactions to grief include a broad range of emotions, behaviors, and physical responses, such as:

- Denial/disbelief
- Anxiety/fear
- Relief
- Shame/guilt
- Sadness
- Loneliness
- Anger/resentment
- Feeling overwhelmed
- Thoughts of suicide
- Inability to make decisions or complete basic tasks
- Change in sleeping pattern
- Increased alcohol consumption
- Change in eating pattern
- Avoidance of people or activities
- Trouble focusing and concentrating

- Crisis of faith
- Body pains or fatigue
- **And anything else.** All grief reactions are normal. However, if you feel someone is in danger of causing harm to themselves or someone else, please seek professional assistance or call 988, the national suicide and crisis helpline.

Different and seemingly contradictory emotions of grief can happen simultaneously. Someone can feel relief, guilt, anger, and sadness, which can be confusing but is normal and expected. When I lost my best friend, I felt sad because I missed her, but I also felt anger about some of her behaviors and guilt about some of mine.

It is common for a recent loss to bring up painful memories and experiences from previous losses. For example, when I made the decision to euthanize my cat, it reminded me of my previous pets and the sadness of losing them. My grief was more complex since I was essentially grieving multiple losses.

Myths of grief

There are many misconceptions and misunderstandings about grief. Here are a few of the most common.

Myth: Grief happens in set-defined linear stages.

The original purpose of Swiss psychiatrist, Elizabeth Kübler-Ross' Five Stages of Grief (denial, anger, bargaining, depression, and acceptance) was to describe how people face their mortality, not how to heal from loss. This model has since been adapted for those in grief, but the stages were never meant to simplify and categorize complex emotional responses to loss. It is normal and expected to have oscillation between many feelings.

Myth: Grief takes a certain period of time to get over.

Everyone grieves differently and at their own pace. Nothing is standard in grief.

Myth: Talking about the loss makes it worse.

The opposite is usually true. Not talking about the loss can make a person feel isolated and alone in their pain.

Myth: Time heals all wounds.

While time can help, it does not heal. Feeling and acknowledging the pain of grief is what heals. For example, when my mother had to be transferred to a facility, I didn't grieve the loss of her health until after my life had settled from addressing her medical, legal, and property affairs. My grief was still waiting for me.

Myth: Being happy dishonors the loss.

Although it is uncomfortable to have moments of joy, it is normal to feel various emotions throughout the grieving process. It is expected to move from feelings of despair and guilt to feelings of hope and joy.

Sometimes there are signs to be seen and ways to prevent suicide. However, some suicides happen unexpectedly, and it can leave loved ones feeling intense shame and guilt about "not seeing the signs." Some suicides happen because the person was resolved on ending their suffering and their loved ones did everything they could.

Acknowledging and validating their emotions and behaviors will allow space for self-compassion, which is helpful for healing.

Myth: Everyone needs to see a grief counselor after a significant loss.

While seeking professional support can be very helpful for some, people can grieve with the love and help of their support system. Inherently, humans seek physical and emotional wholeness when obstacles are removed. However, if some symptoms persist (such as guilt, sadness, anger, nightmares, etc.) or if safety is a concern, a professional may be able to help.

Healing from grief

Healing from a loss happens by experiencing the pain while giving some space for healthy distractions such as exercising, watching shows, chatting with friends, etc. Healing is a challenging process. It has ups and downs, good and bad days, laughs and tears.

People heal in community. They are best supported not by lessening or reframing the pain but by being present with the grief, acknowledging it, and listening. The person grieving is forever changed and needs support to adapt to their life after loss.

WHAT CAN I SAY OR DO TO SUPPORT?

Everyone grieves differently. There is no standard, quick-fix approach to supporting someone who has experienced a painful loss. Relying on what feels comfortable to you is often ineffective and, in some cases, can cause disconnection and more pain. This includes offering familiar phrases that are comfortable for us and what we assume the person grieving wants to hear or needs from us.

The hard truth: You cannot say or do anything to make someone grieving feel their pain any less.

It may seem counterintuitive, but when we make efforts to help someone feel better, it can be invalidating and dismissive. Instead, support them by acknowledging their pain and by listening. It may feel too easy or not enough, but sitting with someone in pain can be challenging. Notice your own discomfort with loss and being around others in pain. Your reaction may be to fix it, please them, or avoid it, which is the opposite of what they need from you. If you struggle with sitting in discomfort, you are not alone. Take a moment to notice your breath and any tension in your body. Sometimes just putting your attention on it can shift it. This is hard work. Remember, they just need you to acknowledge and affirm their experience of grief, not fix them.

"No one reaches out to you for compassion or empathy so you can teach them how to behave better. They reach out to us because they believe in our capacity to know our darkness well enough to sit in the dark with them."

Brené Brown

First and foremost, be genuine. Don't be afraid to say you struggle with emotions or are worried you will say the wrong thing. Here are some examples of expressing your discomfort while still showing support.

> "I'm not good at this sensitive stuff, but I really want to support you the best I can."

> "I don't know what to do or say, but I'm here for you in this and willing to learn what you need from me."

> "I'm worried I will say the wrong thing to you and make things worse, but I want to try to be there for you."

Reach out

Even if you don't know exactly what to say or do and don't get a response back, reach out.

"I'm thinking about you."

"Sending you a hug."

"I am sending you love and prayers."

"I'm so sad to hear about Joe."

"I heard about what happened. How awful."

"Love you."

Continue to reach out

Usually, many supportive people forget with time, but the person grieving doesn't. So keep reaching out. The first anniversaries of special dates can be especially tough.

> *"Hey, I haven't talked to you in a while; can we meet for dinner next week?"*

> *"How are you feeling with Mother's Day coming up?"*

> *"I know today is the anniversary of Bob's death; how are you doing?"*

Offer supportive touch

If you both are okay with it, offer a supportive touch. You can hug them, hold their hand, caress their back, or sit next to them.

> *"Would you like a hug?"*

> *"May I hold your hand?"*

> *"Would you like for me to sit next to you?"*

Empathize and validate their feelings and behaviors. Empathy is not about relating to someone's exact experience; it's about relating to their emotions. Validating is about understanding and expressing acceptance of their emotional experience.

"Yes, this is hard."

"I can understand you feeling hopeless."

"I'd be angry too."

"This just sucks."

*"It's just so f**king unfair."*

"It makes sense you don't want to do anything."

"Of course, you don't want to return home right now."

"It's normal to feel angry **and** sad."

"I get you feeling guilty." (Even when you know they didn't do anything wrong. You are simply validating how they feel.)

Anything that says, "It's okay to feel that way," and "What you are doing is normal."

Talk about the loss

Talk to them about their loss and listen; you don't have to say anything. If they don't want to talk, it's okay to sit in silence with them. Simply being with them can be more powerful than anything you can say in words.

"Want me to come over tonight? We don't have to talk if you don't want to."

"If you are up for it, I would love to share some memories of Mildred."

"Do you want to talk about what happened?"

"What do you most miss about Dudley?"

"Your dad had the best sense of humor."

Ask about their needs

Ask what they need from you. If they don't know (many don't because they are so overwhelmed), offer something you think may be helpful.

> *"Hey, do you want me to drop off dinner this week, or do you want me to come over to spend some time with you?"*

> *"Can I help you with your resume and cover letter? It can be so overwhelming."*

> *"I can pick up the kids for a few hours if that would help you."*

"Is there anything I can do to help? I could take you out of the house for a distraction or go grocery shopping for you."

"Want to come over for dinner tomorrow?"

Offer distractions

Sometimes they need a break from the enormity of their grief. So offer them a distraction.

> "Want a distraction this week? We can go for a walk tomorrow night."

> "You up for joining me for a yoga class this week to get out of the house?"

> "I know you may not feel like it, but do you want to grab some dinner with me Wednesday?"

> "Want to join me for a game of pickleball this weekend?"

Be specific in your questions

Be specific when you ask them how they are doing. Simply asking them, "How are you doing/feeling" can be hard to answer.

*"How are you doing **today**?"*

*"How are you feeling **being here**?"*

*"How has it been the **last two weeks**?"*

*"How is it **going back to work**?"*

Be patient

Be patient with them. If they decline all of your offers, don't take it personally. It may feel like rejection, but they may not be ready yet. Let them know you are available when they are ready.

What can I write in a card or letter?

Express your love and support with authenticity. They might not open your card for weeks or months because facing all the sentiments can be too hard. Here are some examples to put into your own words.

> *"I'm so sad to hear about the passing of..."*

> *"Sending love, thoughts, and prayers to you and your family."*

> *"This sucks..."*

> *"We are saddened to hear about..."*

> *"I'm here if you want to talk, just cry, or anything else you need."*

"Holding you close in my thoughts."

"Wishing you moments of comfort and peace."

"I know how much she meant to you."

"He will be missed. He was an amazing person with a warm heart and smile."

WHAT SHOULD I NOT SAY OR DO?

Even with the best intentions, we can often say things that invalidate, isolate, or shame the grieving person. The previous section introduces helpful things to say and do for those grieving. This section focuses on words and actions that can be hurtful. Specifically, when we actively "try" to help someone feel better, it's hard to be present with them and listen. A typical reaction is to try to fix their pain so they feel better or to avoid it altogether.

Don't avoid

Don't avoid someone grieving. This one may seem obvious, but it can happen when we don't know what to say or are worried about saying the wrong thing. If you learn of a loss, reach out to them, or if you see them in public, acknowledge them.

DO

"I heard about Ron. This is awful."

"I just heard what happened. Can you talk now, or can I call you later today?"

"I'd love to talk when you are up for it."

Don't offer opinions or advice

Don't offer unsolicited opinions or advice. Keep your judgments to yourself. The way they think, how they feel, what they believe, and what they do is expected and normal. (See the list of normal reactions to grief above.)

DON'T

"You should sell your house so you aren't reminded of what happened."

"I think getting another dog soon would be a good idea."

"It's time to move on."

"It's not that bad."

"You shouldn't feel guilty about that."

"You should be grateful for what you have."

"You need to get back to work to stay busy."

"Aren't you drinking too much?"

Any message that conveys *"You shouldn't feel that way"* or *"You are doing something wrong."*

Don't offer trite sayings

Don't try to pacify their emotions with trite sayings to help them see the "bright side" of the situation. They may come to that conclusion for themselves, but if you say it to them, it can invalidate and dismiss their pain.

DON'T

"He is in a better place."

"It was her time to go."

"At least they aren't suffering anymore."

"God must have had a different plan for her."

"God called him home."

"Things happen for a reason."

"Time heals all wounds."

"God only gives you what you can handle."

Don't tell your loss stories

Don't tell long, detailed stories about your own loss and grief unless they ask. It takes the focus from them onto you. You can mention you had a similar loss if you think that may help validate their pain and experience.

DON'T

"I lost my mother three years ago. It was so hard for me because she was my best friend, and I didn't know what to do. I was her caretaker for two years because she was..."

DO

"I understand you feeling some relief when your dad died. I felt something similar when I lost my mom."

"I get why you are still in shock. It took me a year to feel normal after my divorce."

"When I lost Max, I was angry all the time, but it did get better with time and talking about it."

Don't sympathize

Don't be sympathetic. Sympathy is not the same as empathy or compassion. Sympathy is feeling sorry for someone else. It keeps you at a safe distance from their pain and conveys disconnection and pity.

DON'T

"I feel sorry for you."

"I wouldn't be able to handle this situation."

"You poor thing."

"I'm so sorry for you."

"I can't imagine what you are going through." (They actually want you to imagine their pain so that you can understand their experience.)

DO

"I'm so sorry for your loss."

"I'm sorry this happened to you."

"I can only imagine what it is like losing a child. Tell me what you are going through."

Just listen.

Refer to *Empathize* section from the previous chapter for more examples.

Don't assume

Don't assume their emotions and thoughts about the loss. Even if you had a similar loss, they might have a very different experience. For example, you may have been best friends with your mother, while they may have had an abusive relationship with theirs.

DON'T

"You must be devastated by the loss of your mother."

"I know exactly how you feel; I lost my husband too."

"I bet you are so relieved about your divorce!"

DO

"Were you close with your mother?"

"I felt lost and scared when my husband died a few years ago; tell me about your experience."

"How are you feeling at this point in your divorce?"

Don't compare

Don't compare your loss with theirs; it is invalidating and implies their pain isn't as important.

DON'T

"I lost my father when I was young; at least you had him most of your life."

"At least you got to say goodbye; my husband died in a car accident."

"You should be grateful for your severance; I got nothing when I was laid off."

Don't ask about the cause of death

Don't ask how a person died; it can be a sensitive subject. It could have been a long, painful death, a tragic accident, a suicide, or murder. If they want you to know, they will tell you.

DON'T

"He was so young; what happened?"

"What did she die from?"

"Was it cancer?"

If you learned someone died from a "preventable cause" (lung cancer, car crash, suicide, substance abuse, etc.), don't comment or ask questions about their lifestyle choices because it can insult the deceased.

DON'T

"I heard it was lung cancer. Did he smoke?"

"How often did he go to the doctor?"

"Was he wearing his seatbelt?"

"Did she get regular mammograms?"

"Well, he was an addict, so what can you expect?"

"Was she overweight?"

"He was so selfish to take his own life."

Don't ask about their plans

Don't ask what they plan to do, especially in the beginning. It can feel like pressure when they may be struggling with making decisions.

DON'T

"Are you going to start trying for another baby soon?"

"Do you think you will sell the house?"

"How long are you going to take a leave from work?"

SPECIAL CASES

Their loss triggers your grief

If you have experienced a recent similar loss and talking to someone grieving about their loss is too difficult or painful for you, let them know and share with them how you are comfortable supporting them.

Losses by suicide

If the loss is by suicide, it comes with a broader range and intensity of emotions and reactions, but all these guidelines still apply.

If you are worried about their behaviors

If you are worried about their excessive drinking, spending, isolation, or any other non-life-threatening behavior, it is best not to bring it up with them unless they bring it up as a concern. These behaviors are ways to have moments of relief from the pain and usually will resolve with the healing process. If you are concerned about dangerous behaviors such as drunk driving or statements about hurting themselves, seek professional assistance or call 988, the national suicide and crisis helpline.

CONCLUSION

If all of this sounds too confusing and you are worried you keep doing the "wrong" thing, the actual expert is the person grieving. These are basic guidelines that may or may not apply to every person. Take their lead and use your best judgment based on your knowledge of them. Ask them if you want to know if something is offensive or invalidating. Be open to their feedback and show you are trying. Sometimes that is all it takes.

"The most useful asset of a person is not a head full of knowledge but a heart full of love, with ears open to listen, and hands willing to help."

Unknown

Cheat Sheet

Intention: Be a loving support.

Reminder: It is hard work to sit with someone in pain. Notice your discomfort and breathe.

DO

Listen.

Acknowledge.

Validate (accept their experience).

DON'T

Avoid their pain.

Fix or lessen their pain.

Give advice or judgments.

RESOURCES

For an updated and more comprehensive list of resources, go to www.howtosupportgrief.com.

Phone numbers

988

National Suicide and Crisis Lifeline

211

A comprehensive source of information about local resources and social services

www.sprc.org

Suicide Prevention Resource Center

www.211.org

A comprehensive source of information about local resources and social services

www.grief.com

Comprehensive resource on grief

www.griefshare.org

Grief support groups

www.hospicefoundation.org

Hospice Foundation

Books

On Grief and Grieving: Finding the Meaning of Grief Through the Five Stages of Loss by Elisabeth Kübler-Ross and David Kessler

It's OK That You're Not OK: Meeting Grief and Loss in a Culture That Doesn't Understand by Megan Devine and Mark Nepo

The Other Side of Sadness: What the New Science of Bereavement Tells Us About Life After Loss by George Bonanno

The 4 Facets of Grief: Heal Your Heart, Rebuild Your World, and Find New Pathways to Joy by Ruth E. Field

Finding Peace When Your Heart Is In Pieces: A Step-by-Step Guide to the Other Side of Grief, Loss, and Pain by Paul Coleman

Opening to Grief: Finding Your Way from Loss to Peace by Claire B. Willis and Marnie Crawford Samuelson

Podcasts

All There Is with Anderson Cooper

Healing with David Kessler